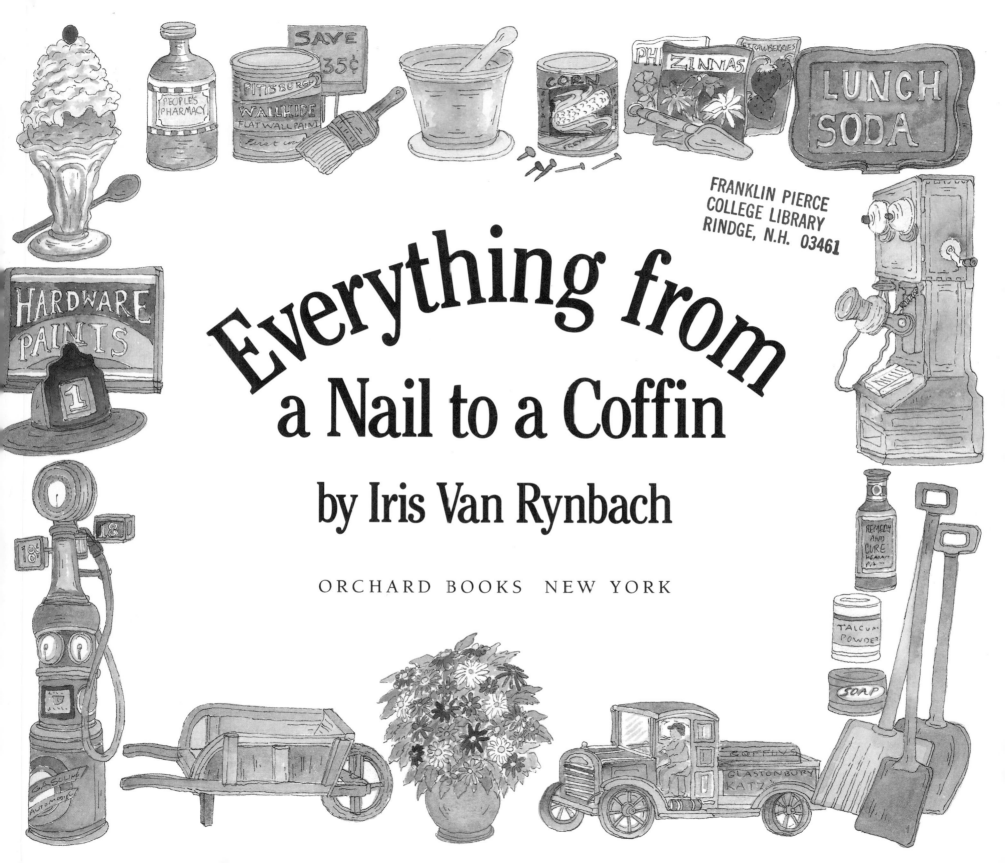

Everything from
a Nail to a Coffin

by Iris Van Rynbach

ORCHARD BOOKS   NEW YORK

Glastonbury is a real town in Connecticut, and this book tells the true story of one of its buildings and some of its citizens. For source material, the author spoke with people who knew this building and the families who lived and worked in it over the years. She also looked at land deeds, purchase and sale contracts, and other records on file at the Historical Society of Glastonbury and the town clerk's office of Glastonbury. She used photographs from the Historical Society of Glastonbury and the New York Public Library. In addition, the following two books provided background information on late-nineteenth- and early-twentieth-century Glastonbury: *Glastonbury: From Settlement to Suburb* by Marjorie Grant McNulty (1983, Historical Society of Glastonbury) and *The Glastonbury Express* by Daniel T. Heddon (1983, produced in cooperation with the Historical Society of Glastonbury).

Many thanks to Adeline Greenburg, Dick and Betsy Katz, Harvey Katz, and Frank Muccio, who shared with me their stories and memories. And for help and guidance in researching old town records, thanks to Doris Armstead, Marjorie McNulty, and Nancy Berlet at the Glastonbury Historical Society.

Orchard Books, A division of Franklin Watts, Inc., 387 Park Avenue South, New York, NY 10016

Manufactured in Hong Kong. Printed and bound by Toppan Printing Company, Inc. Book design by Jean Krulis.

10 9 8 7 6 5 4 3 2 1

The text of this book is set in 16 pt. Berkeley Oldstyle Medium. The illustrations are watercolor with pen-and-ink.

Library of Congress Cataloging-in-Publication Data
Van Rynbach, Iris. Everything from a nail to a coffin / Iris Van Rynbach.   p.   cm.   Summary: Traces the ownership and development of a retail establishment in Glastonbury, Connecticut, thus reflecting life in the town between 1874 and the present.   ISBN 0-531-05941-3.—ISBN 0-531-08541-4   1. Stores, Retail—Connecticut—Glastonbury—History—Juvenile literature.   2. Glastonbury (Conn.)—Social life and customs—Juvenile literature.   [1. Stores, Retail—Connecticut—Glastonbury—History. 2. Glastonbury (Conn.)—Social life and customs.]
I. Title.   HF5429.5.G53V36   1991   381'.1'097462—dc20   90-23035

FOR MICHAEL

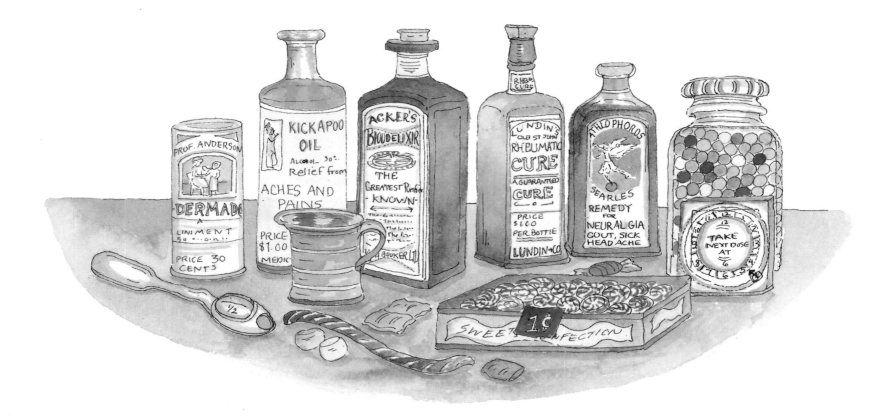

Edwards and Henry Goodrich are planning to
open a store. It will be called the Goodrich General Store. Big windows in front will display their goods. Upstairs there will be apartments for people to live in.

The two brothers buy ten acres of land on which to build. The land, once used for farming, costs them three thousand dollars. They buy it from Joseph Porter in the fall of 1874.

The following spring a big hole is dug. The foundation is laid with fieldstone and mortar. The frame of the building is made from local trees. A large chestnut beam runs down the middle. Planks are nailed to the framework, and wood clapboard is nailed to the planks. Around the base of the building the Goodriches use brick as decoration.

There is a slanted, or pitched, roof with shingles made of wood. There are three steps up from the road to the front door and a granite hitching post out front for tying up horses. Inside the walls are lined with wood lathing, or thin wood strips, that are covered with plaster. Dozens of shelves are put up. Finally everything is ready!

The Goodrich General Store is located right on Main Street in the town of Glastonbury, Connecticut. Main Street is a wide, unpaved road that follows the Connecticut River. The road is lined with tall elm and maple trees and big homes built after the town was first settled in 1636. Beyond the houses are meadows and fields.

In the late 1800s Glastonbury is already a thriving town, and there are a few other stores on Main Street. There is also a post office, a town hall built of red brick, and a wooden schoolhouse with separate entrances marked BOYS and GIRLS. Along the road people are traveling on horseback, by stagecoach, and in horse-drawn buggies. Outside of town are companies and mills that make soap, leather goods, and wool and cotton thread.

Edwards and Henry Goodrich, or the Goodrich brothers, plan to sell many kinds of goods in their store, including shaving soap and talcum powder from the J. B. Williams Company factory in town. There will be crates of local peaches in the summer from Hale's Fruit Farm. Coffee, tea, butter, cheese, oats, and candy are also for sale.

People usually come into town once a week to shop. Mrs. Mosley stops by on a hot July day for six dozen eggs; she is baking this week. Altogether the eggs cost $1.08. Henry Goodrich uses a crow quill pen to write down the sale of goods in his large leather book, noting the date and how much money was spent.

A few years later, in 1879, Edwards decides to try his hand at tobacco farming and sells his half of the store and land to his brother Henry for one dollar.

For several years Henry runs the store, and business is good. But eventually he too decides to sell out and try his hand at a new business. Right down the street from his old general store, he forms the Riverside Manufacturing Company, where he makes paperboard and sells coal. On April 19, 1888, Henry sells the store and the land to Hattie and Sturges Turner.

Hattie and Sturges have a plan to open People's Pharmacy in the old Goodrich General Store building. First they remodel and put up a new sign out front. It is the first pharmacy in town—with the town's first pay telephone! Mr. Oatrum, and in later years Mr. Dinsmore, mixes "compounds" to fill prescriptions in its dispensary. Wild cherry cough drops for five cents and boxes of medicine for rheumatism are for sale.

People's Pharmacy also has a soda fountain equipped to make all sorts of ice cream dishes. One of the town favorites is a Dusty Monday, made with vanilla ice cream, chocolate malted milk powder, whipped cream, and a cherry on top!

Mr. and Mrs. Turner run their business for nearly ten years before deciding to lease out part of the building to Frank Lee. Mr. Turner is Frank Lee's guardian, so the price for leasing is cheap—only one dollar. Frank wants to open his own general store, and Mr. Turner will continue to run People's Pharmacy next door.

Soon Frank has his shelves stocked with a wide variety of goods, from shoes to bolts of colored cloth. Brooms are stacked in empty flour barrels, handle-end down; other barrels are filled with flour and sugar. Rows of glass jars hold penny candy. Many of the supplies are from local mills and farms; other goods come from Hartford or have been shipped up the river by steamboat from New York. In the window Mr. Lee posts a sign:

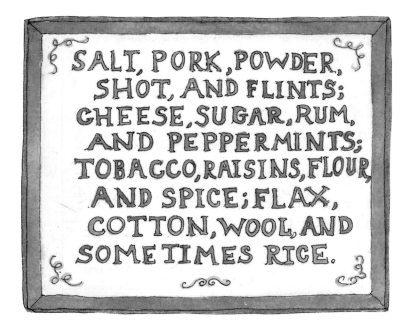

SALT, PORK, POWDER, SHOT, AND FLINTS; CHEESE, SUGAR, RUM, AND PEPPERMINTS; TOBACCO, RAISINS, FLOUR AND SPICE; FLAX, COTTON, WOOL, AND SOMETIMES RICE.

Behind the store is a stable where the horses and carriages are kept. Groceries and other goods from the store are packed into wooden crates and delivered daily by horse-drawn carriage.

Mr. Lee hires a man named George Howard to help out. Mr. Howard works in the store for many years, and he also makes the delivery rounds. He often stops along the way to exchange news or have a cup of coffee in a customer's kitchen.

Frank Lee himself works in the store every day. His wife and their daughter Irene often come in to visit and help out. Other families make a weekly outing of coming to town to shop; they arrive in hand-pulled wagons in the summer and sleds in the winter. The children often ride on the way in, but groceries take their place going home. Children seldom leave without a piece of candy.

Over the next ten years electricity is introduced to most of the homes and businesses in town. Big new homes are built, and the town grows. A few cars are now seen on Main Street, including an early Model T Ford.

By 1910 the road in front of the store has been paved, and a sidewalk has been built of cinder ash from the coal furnaces. A trolley runs down Main Street several times a day, stopping right in front of Frank Lee's store—Station 33. The trolley costs five cents a ride.

Upstairs in the second floor apartment over the stores live the family of James McEvoy. Their rent is four dollars a month. James goes to work for Frank in the store. One of his jobs is to deliver ice to the customers by horse-drawn wagon. In the winter large blocks of ice are cut from local ponds and stored in an icehouse all year long. The icehouse has thick walls insulated with sawdust to keep the ice frozen.

In the early 1900s millions of immigrants from southern and eastern Europe move to the United States. Some of the old farms in Glastonbury are purchased by these newcomers after the original owners move west or into the cities. One of the original farms that continues to prosper is Hale's, started by two young brothers from a small strawberry bed and a few seedling peach trees. Tobacco is still grown locally, just as it was by Edwards Goodrich. In the fields are long, low tobacco barns with open sides so that the tobacco can dry.

In 1918, at the end of World War I, a big celebration parade takes place on Main Street. There are flags flying, marching bands, and soldiers in full uniform. Children throw bouquets of flowers as the soldiers march by.

In 1920, the same year women are given the right to vote, Mr. and Mrs. Turner decide to sell their whole building to Frank Lee. They have been in business for thirty years. Soon after Frank buys the building, however, he decides to move to California to live with his daughter Irene. So he sells the store to a father and son from New Britain, Connecticut—Ben and Joseph Katz.

Ben and Joe plan to open their own business, similar to the stores run by the Turners and Frank Lee. People's Pharmacy soon becomes the Katz Soda Shop. And Frank Lee's General Store becomes B. Katz and Son, Groceries. The Katzes paint the outside of the building gray to give it a fresh look. And the soda fountain is remodeled with a long marble countertop, stools in front, and a large, shiny mirror behind.

In the grocery store the Katzes sell Royal Scarlet Brand vegetables and fruits in cans, along with bread and milk and fresh produce. A can of Pork and Beans costs five cents. They also sell hardware—rakes, shovels, hammers, gardening tools, and kerosene heaters. There are long cases filled with overalls, work shirts, boots, and socks in all sizes. Wheelbarrows, washbasins, and ladders are for sale. The store slogan is

EVERYTHING FROM A NAIL TO A COFFIN

The Katzes have a family dog named Mak, who often roams around the store, looking for scraps. He is part terrier and part cocker spaniel. Ben's wife, Rose, loves to garden. From her beds behind the store she brings in bouquets of fresh flowers to decorate the countertop near the register.

In the window of the Katz Soda Shop a sign advertises CONFECTIONARY AND ICE CREAM. Inside the store a large case is filled with trays of penny candy, peppermints, chocolates, Tootsie Rolls, and butterscotch bonbons. There are racks filled with magazines, the *Police Gazette*, and local newspapers like the *Hartford Courant*. Behind the counter a two-burner gas stove is used to make hot sandwiches. Sparkling-clean dishes and glasses are lined up, ready for ice cream sundaes and milk shakes. There are large bowls of sundae toppings made daily by Rose Katz—including tutti-frutti and hot fudge—and silver soda fountains for seltzer.

The shop also has several small round "ice cream" tables with chairs. Rose and Ben's daughter Adeline comes home from school to do her homework on one of these. Other children ride their bikes or walk from school to have a scoop of Besse's Brand ice cream or a Cherry Smash. Adeline helps sweep the store by tossing sawdust on the floor, and oil on top of that to hold down the dust. This turns the sawdust green! On Sunday afternoons families often come in together for soda or ice cream.

By the end of the 1920s the stock market crash has brought on the Great Depression. Many people lose their jobs and are out of work. The Katz family remains in business, and they extend credit to some of their customers who can't pay their bills all at once.

Ben and Joe belong to the Volunteer Fire Department. When there's a fire, the townspeople call a special telephone number that rings in the grocery store. Then Ben presses a button in the back of the store that sounds the fire alarm outside, to call the volunteer firemen, including Ben and Joe, to duty. Across the street from the store is the hose house, where they hook up the hoses and pump water.

On Friday nights many of the older men in town drop by to visit Ben and listen to the Friday night fights on the radio. A championship fight by Joe Louis always draws a big crowd.

At other times there are wood chopping contests, sponsored by the Collins Ax Company of Collinsville, Connecticut, out in back of the store. The person who chops the most logs wins a brand-new ax!

In 1936, after very heavy rains, the Connecticut River overflows its banks, and the town of Glastonbury is flooded. The townspeople have some advance warning, so Ben and Joe are able to move goods upstairs from the basement and escape a lot of damage. At the height of the flood the store has four feet of water in it!

Two years later a terrible hurricane hits the town with winds of one hundred miles per hour. Many of the big old trees along Main Street are lost, and the steeple of the Congregational church is ripped down.

By the late 1930s the store has undergone many changes. The front of the building has been enclosed, there is now only one entrance, and the three steps from the street are now inside the enlarged front entryway. Groceries are delivered in an open bed truck or a Reo speed wagon (later on in a Dodge truck). The horses and carriages are gone, and the granite hitching post out in front of the store has been replaced by a hand crank gasoline pump. Cars like Fords and Packards are parked on Main Street. The icehouse business has been closed.

During World War II, from 1941 to 1945, many local men and women volunteer or are drafted into the Army, Navy, or Air Force. The whole country gets behind the war effort. Since supplies are short, rationing is introduced. Shoe rationing begins in 1943; later meat, cheese, fats, and canned goods are rationed as well. Each family can purchase only a certain amount of gasoline each month. The rest of the shoes and food and gasoline is allotted to the armed services.

During the years following the war, Glastonbury begins to change from a rural town to a suburban one. In East Hartford, a few miles away, a large aircraft manufacturing plant opens and hires many people. Servicemen coming home from the war start families and need homes. The old farmland is turned into subdivision housing as the population grows. New schools are built. Along Main Street some of the old homes are being restored, while others have fallen into disrepair.

All of these changes lead to a change in the Katz family business. By 1955 Ben's grandson Dick Katz is in charge of the store. There are other grocery stores being built in town. So Dick decides to combine the soda shop and the grocery store into one larger business. It will be called Katz Hardware.

First Dick remodels the building. He replaces the large display windows with picture windows across the front of the building. The outside walls of wood clapboard are painted yellow, and a new shingle roof is added. In each section of the new windows are displays of paint, rakes, shovels, and hardware.

Inside there is one large open space with many shelves stocked with cans of paint, seeds for vegetables, flashlights, and gardening tools. Fishing and hunting gear and other sporting goods, kitchen supplies, mailboxes, and gas-powered lawn mowers are also to be found. A small counter near the entrance holds the cash register.

Dick hires a young man named Howard Mason. Howard has gone to Hartford High School with one of the Katz cousins. Two days after Howard graduates, he goes to work in the store and remains employed there for the rest of his life. The whole town gets to know him well.

The trolley cars are now gone on Main Street. It is paved in asphalt with white lines down the center, a traffic light stands on the corner, and Oldsmobiles, wood-paneled station wagons, and pickup trucks drive by in front of the store. Many of the old buildings are being torn down, and new shops and a supermarket are being built. Some of the old houses are converted for offices and businesses.

During the 1970s, there are many social changes in the country. Students march in protest against the Vietnam War. Dick Katz decides to make a change for himself and sells the family business to a man named Larry Schakett. Dick then opens up a decorating business. But four years later he buys the store back from Larry Schakett and is behind the counter of Katz Hardware once again.

Main Street is still the center of town. Outside of town much of the farmland has been developed into condominium complexes, more houses, offices, and small shopping centers. Less tobacco is now grown locally, and many of the old tobacco barns have fallen into disrepair. A highway connects Glastonbury to Hartford, and rush hour traffic clogs the road. Fast food restaurants are opening. But new trees have been planted along Main Street to replace those lost in the hurricane of 1938, and almost all the old colonial homes are now beautifully restored.

In the late 1980s the Katz Hardware building is remodeled again. The smaller windows of earlier times are restored, and the outside is painted white with black shutters. Inside the store you can buy a shop-vac, a bug zapper, a leaf blower, tulip bulbs, and a paintbrush. The sidewalk is filled with displays of wheelbarrows, bags of fertilizer, and ladders. And a new sign hangs outside:

KATZ HARDWARE LAWN AND GARDEN

Dick Katz is behind the cash register. Working with him is his stepson Bob Krieger. Hanging on the wall behind them are framed photographs of People's Pharmacy; Frank Lee's General Store; Dick's grandparents, Rose and Ben; and Dick's parents, Lucy and Joe.

The population of Glastonbury has grown from about three thousand five hundred in the 1870s to about twenty-nine thousand in the 1990s. Main Street is now two lanes wider, and there is a pedestrian walk light to guide people through the traffic. Instead of the one room schoolhouse of 1890, there are now five large elementary schools. There are several modern firehouses, each with its own fire trucks. And there are a half-dozen stores where you can buy a milk shake or an ice cream soda. But despite all these changes, more than a hundred years after it was built, there is still a shop on Main Street, where the Goodrich General Store once stood, that stocks the variety of goods that inspired the earlier Katzes' slogan:

EVERYTHING FROM A NAIL TO A COFFIN